A Painful History of Medicine

Bedpans, Blood + Bandages

a history of hospitals

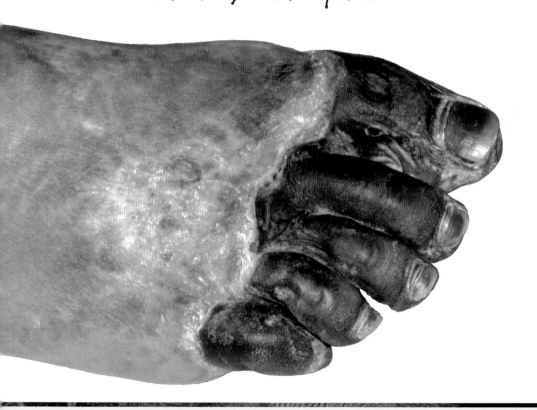

John Townsend

www.raintreepublishers.co.uk

Visit our website to find out more information about **Raintree** books.

To order:
☎ Phone 44 (0) 1865 888113
📄 Send a fax to 44 (0) 1865 314091
💻 Visit the Raintree bookshop at **www.raintreepublishers.co.uk** to browse our catalogue and order online.

First published in Great Britain by Raintree, Halley Court, Jordan Hill, Oxford OX2 8EJ, part of Harcourt Education.
Raintree is a registered trademark of Harcourt Education Ltd.

Editorial: Melanie Copland
and Kate Buckingham
Design: Michelle Lisseter
and Bridge Creative Services Ltd
Picture Research: Hannah Taylor
and Ginny Stroud-Lewis
Production: Duncan Gilbert
Originated by Dot Gradations
Printed and bound in China
by South China Printing Company

ISBN 1 844 43752 3
09 08 07 06 05
10 9 8 7 6 5 4 3 2 1

British Library Cataloguing in Publication Data

Townsend, John
Hospitals – (A Painful History of Medicine)
362.1'1'09
A full catalogue record for this book is available from the British Library.

Acknowledgements

Alamy Images pp. **36–37** (Popperfoto), **42** (David Wall), **45** (Steve Allen, Brand X Pictures), **48–49** (AGStockUSA, Inc. Ed Young), **48** (Comstock Images); Art Directors and Trip pp. **13**, **17**; Corbis pp. **10–11** (Underwood & Underwood), **11** (Sygma/ Jacques Langevin), **12** (Historical Picture Archive), **12–13** (Anthony Bannister/ Gallo Images), **14** (Michael Nicholson), **14–15**, **16–17** (Michael Maslan Historic Photographs), **18–19**, **26** (Peter Turnley), **26–27** (Hulton-Deutsch Collection), **32** (Bettmann), **34**, **37** (Swim Ink), **38–39** (Tim Fisher/ The Military Picture Library), **39** (Bettmann), **40** (Kit Kittle), **41** (Yann Arthus-Bertrand), **42–43** (Jonathan Blair), **44–45** (Dusko Despotovic); Getty Images pp. **50–51**; Hulton Archive pp. **31**, **33**, **38**; Mary Evans Picture Library pp. **23**, **24**, **25**, **29**; Medical on Line pp. **6**, **22–23**; Science Photo Library pp. **19** (National Library of Medicine), **20** (Sinclair Stammers), **20–21** (Jean-Loup Charmet), **21** (Mike Devlin), **43** (Ed Young), **46** (Cal Goetgheluck), **46–47** (Volker Steger), **47** (Geoff Tompkinson); Sylvia Cordaiy p. **15**; The Art Archive/ Imperial War Museum, London pp. **34–35**; The Kobal Collection pp. **6–7** (MGM), **8–9** (Dreamworks/ Universal/ Buitendijk, Jaap), **30**, **50**; The Royal College of Surgeons pp. **4–5**; Topham Picturepoint p. **28**; Wellcome Library, London pp. **9**, **30–31**, **35**.

Disclaimer

Contents

Any words appearing in the text in bold,
like this, are explained in the glossary.
You can also look out for them in the Word
bank at the bottom of each page.

Ouch!

Two hundred years ago, some doctors thought hospitals were a bad idea. Hospitals then were not very clean. Diseases spread easily. But now we know how to stop diseases spreading, hospitals are the best places for sick people!

A hospital was once a place to fear. Just the word was enough to bring shivers of panic. It was the last place anyone dared to go. Hospitals had disgusting smells, filthy rats and messy **bedpans**.

Patients cried out with pain from infected wounds. Dirty bandages oozed with slimy **pus**. Even doctors felt sick at the sight and smell of wounds and disease. If you felt ill, hospitals would make you feel far worse. A hospital was often the last place a patient ever saw.

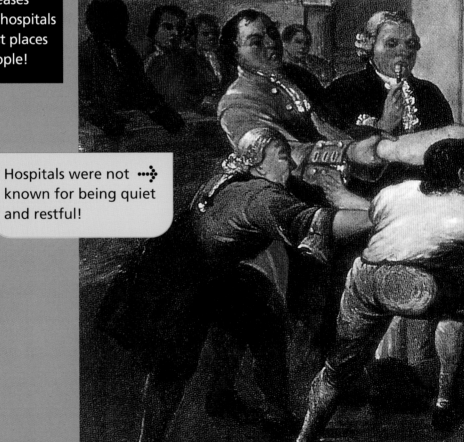

Hospitals were not ···› known for being quiet and restful!

Word bank

bedpan   shallow pan used as a toilet by someone who cannot get out of bed

Times have changed

Hospitals have come a long way since those days! Today they are places where great skill can save lives. The knowledge gained over hundreds of years is used to treat very ill people. A modern hospital is full of the latest amazing technology.

Today's hospitals are a world away from the **wards** of years ago. There may still be bedpans, bandages and blood – but there is nothing like the misery of the past.

Find out later...

Why were there rats in some hospitals?

Why were some hospitals in the middle of fields?

Why are there still maggots in hospitals?

pus   thick yellow or greenish foul-smelling liquid made by infected wounds

Nowhere to go

For thousands of years, ancient people carried out basic **surgery**. But special places where the ordinary man or woman could go to be nursed were not built until after Roman times. Hospitals as we know them today with **specialist wards** are quite a new idea.

Today we think of hospitals as large buildings where patients are treated and nursed back to health. But hospitals have only been like this for a few hundred years. The Greeks and the Romans had very different ideas.

Greeks

In ancient Greece, sick people were cared for at home. If they were lucky, they might have a visit from a "healer" who used herbs or honey as medicine. To treat some illnesses they would massage the patient with wine, salt and mustard. There was very little proper care.

Greeks and Romans were used to cutting open patients' boils like this one.

Word bank

infirm   weak
specialist   expert in one particular area

Romans

The Romans took their health seriously. They believed clean water, clean bodies and exercise were good for health. They were right!

Roman doctors tried to treat ill people but some charged high fees. This gave them a bad name.

Slaves were very common in Roman times. At the beginning of the first century AD, a third of all people in Italy were slaves. If they became ill, they were often left to manage on their own. But some rich slave-owners built rooms on their land where doctors could care for them.

Roman slaves had tough lives, with little help if they got hurt or ill.

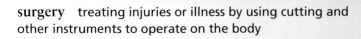

surgery   treating injuries or illness by using cutting and other instruments to operate on the body

Roman soldiers

Augustus was a Roman emperor who lived until AD 14. His army had over 400,000 soldiers. If soldiers were hurt in battles, they were often left behind to die. But Augustus decided to look after any soldiers that were injured.

Augustus built a hospital in a **fort** in Germany in about AD 9. The sick and injured were brought into a large hall, which was also used for **surgery**. But this was strictly for soldiers. It was hundreds of years before ordinary people could be treated in places like this.

Gladiators often got wounded and needed nursing.

Word bank

fort building like a castle, able to withstand enemy attack

Fighting wounds

Historians have found out a lot about Roman hospitals by digging up their ruins. Many medical instruments have been dug up at some sites.

Gladiators were paid to fight each other to entertain the Romans. Some became very famous. Others were wounded and needed to be treated by doctors. Hospitals were used for treating gladiators whose insides had to be put back and bodies stitched up.

This drawing shows a wounded gladiator.

Did you know?

The word hospital was not used until the 14th century. It came from *hospitalis*, the Latin word for guest. Our word hospitality also comes from this. The sick and injured were guests at a place of medical care.

Early Christians

Jerusalem is a city in Israel where Jesus Christ first taught his followers about caring for the poor and the sick. **Christians** in the first century AD began to build places in Jerusalem where ordinary people could go to be treated if they were ill.

Christians set up **hostels** in many different countries where ill people could go. This was the start of hospitals for everyone. At last the sick could go somewhere to be looked after.

Rest houses

In Roman times, **pilgrims** walked hundreds of kilometres to visit the city of Jerusalem. People who lived nearby built hostels to give travellers rest and care.

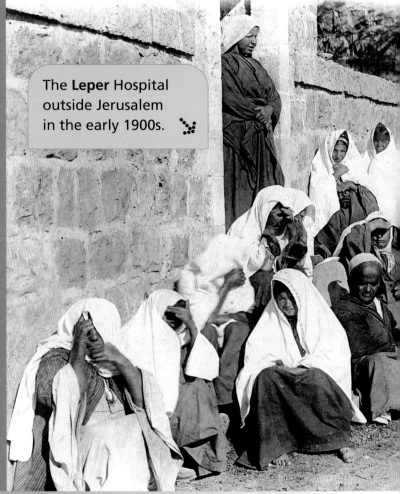

The **Leper** Hospital outside Jerusalem in the early 1900s.

Word bank   **Christian**   follower of Jesus Christ and the religion based on his teachings

The first big hospitals

By AD 550 there was a 200-bed hospital in Jerusalem. Even bigger hospitals in Greece did minor **surgery** for some patients. As the Christian world grew, so did the number of hospitals.

People from other religions also put health and caring at the centre of their work. **Muslim** hospitals started in the 8th century. These were based on the teaching of the **prophet** Muhammad. He was born in AD 570 in Mecca, Arabia. His followers believed that caring for the body was an important part of their faith.

Hospitals in the Middle East

The first Muslim hospital is thought to have opened in Damascus, Syria, in 707 AD. Another was built in Baghdad in 805 AD. By the year 1200, there were more than 35 large hospitals in **Islamic** countries.

A modern hospital in Saudi Arabia.

Muslim   follower of the religion of Islam
prophet   religious leader and teacher

The **Middle Ages** was a time of new ideas about medicine.

Monks

Many **Islamic** medical ideas spread to **Christian monasteries** in Europe. These were where monks lived. They grew plants to make their own medicines. Most monasteries had special rooms where doctor monks could look after sick monks.

Monks also gave shelter to tired **pilgrims**, the sick, the weak and the old. Some monasteries had rooms with about twelve to fifteen beds. Large beds would often hold three people.

Blood

The ancient Greeks carried out blood-letting. It was also done throughout the Middle Ages and even up to recent times.

People thought getting rid of some blood would help to keep down a fever!

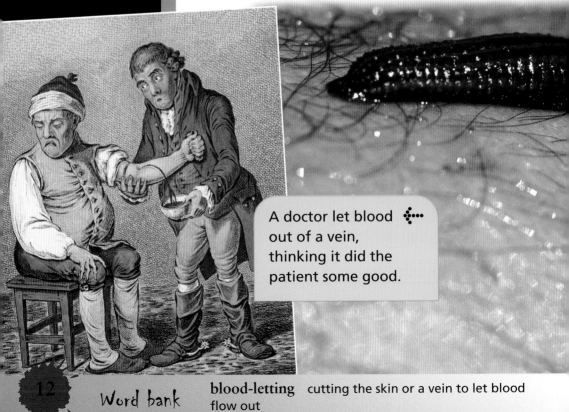

A doctor let blood out of a vein, thinking it did the patient some good.

Word bank **blood-letting** cutting the skin or a vein to let blood flow out

Bleeding

Sometimes there was a separate room in the monastery for **blood-letting**. For centuries people believed that many illnesses were caused by having too much blood. They thought blood should be drained away. Patients would have their arms cut and their blood was collected in a bowl.

Blood-letting could be dangerous, especially if someone was ill to begin with or if their wounds became infected.

Sometimes **leeches** were used to suck blood from a patient's body. The leeches would suck the skin and slowly begin to swell up with blood.

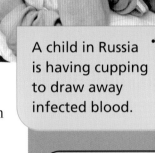

A child in Russia is having cupping to draw away infected blood.

Cupping

Warm cups were sometimes used to draw blood to the surface of the body. They were pushed on to cut skin and the blood was then collected in the cups. Cupping was usually done on the **temples**, behind the ears and at the base of the spine.

A leech ready to drink some blood.

Middle Ages   period of history roughly between AD 500 and AD 1500

City hospitals

Hospitals were built in the main cities of Europe from the 12th century. They were run by monks and nuns and had strict rules. When patients first went into hospital, their clothes were taken away to be washed and mended. The patients were often put into bed naked and made to share the bed with someone else.

There were two main meals a day, served at a table. Very sick people were fed in bed. Most hospitals had a separate kitchen but some meals were prepared in the **wards**.

St John's Hospital in Bruges was one of the oldest hospitals in the world when it closed in 1978.

More than 800 years ago

A few of Europe's hospitals from the **Middle Ages** are still standing today. One is St John's Hospital in Bruges, Belgium (above). It was built in 1188, and is now a hospital museum.

Rats ran around patients in many hospitals.

Word bank   insane   person with mental-health problems

Cats and rats

The scraps of food and dirt around hospital beds were ideal for hungry rats. Cats were kept to kill the mice and rats running around the wards.

Surgery was still very basic. The main treatments included a healthy diet, **blood-letting** and cupping.

Some people were not allowed anywhere near the hospitals. Children, very old people, **lepers** and **insane** people were kept well away.

More than 700 years ago

One of Italy's first city hospitals was built in Florence and is called Santa Maria (below). It opened in 1288 with only 12 beds. Two hundred years later it had 250 beds, 10 doctors, several surgeons and a **pharmacist**. It is still a hospital today.

Santa Maria Nuova in Florence, Italy.

leper   person suffering from leprosy, a terrible skin disease

15

Leprosy

Before modern medicine there was no cure for leprosy. Victims' skin became scaly and infected. Their noses, fingers and toes broke off and they often went blind.

Leprosy was a very **infectious** disease. People shouted names or threw stones to keep victims away.

Lepers were forced to shave their heads and wear a yellow cross to warn people to keep clear. They also had to ring a bell and shout "unclean" to make sure no one came near and caught the dreaded disease from them.

The dreaded disease

Leprosy has struck fear into humans for thousands of years. Victims were often thought to be evil and they were made to live away from other people. Lepers in the USA were shipped to Kalawao in Hawaii. This was set up as a leper colony in 1866.

Lepers could only beg and hope to be given scraps of food.

Word bank antibiotic substance made from bacteria that kills other harmful bacteria

Asylums

In the year 1000 AD there was a leprosy **epidemic** in Europe. It lasted over 200 years.

From 1100 AD, people with leprosy were put in leper houses or **asylums**. These were built outside towns to give shelter and food but not much medical help. Nursing care was given by other lepers or by monks. By 1225, there were almost 20,000 leper asylums across Europe.

It was not until 1873 that the cause of leprosy was found to be a type of **bacteria**. A real cure came in the late 1940s with **antibiotics**.

Leprosy can cover the body in sores.

Did you know?

The word asylum was first used in the 15th century. It meant a place where people could be sheltered and protected. During the **Middle Ages**, lepers needed all the help they could get.

epidemic outbreak of a disease that spreads quickly over a wide area

Tough times

The mind

In 1247, a hospital for "lunatics" was started in London. It was called Bedlam (right). The hospital attracted hundreds of visitors who paid to stare at patients kept in cages like animals in a zoo.

Times were hard if you ended up in hospital between 1500 and 1800. There was still not much that could be done for the sick and injured. You could expect a bed to rest in with meals provided. But treatment, drugs and **surgery** were still very risky.

No one knew about **bacteria** yet. Bacteria spread easily between patients and caused infection. The only way doctors could treat infected arms and legs was to chop them off. The **trauma** of a stay in hospital often affected patients' minds.

Fast facts

The word *luna* means moon. People believed the cycles of the moon affected behaviour. Patients were called lunatics if their behaviour seemed strange.

Word bank

demon	evil spirit or devil
lunatic	name given to a person who was mentally ill

Mental illness

When stress or disease stops our brains from working properly, we may need treatment for mental illness. People with mental illness have been treated badly throughout history.

Lunatic asylums were set up as early as 1247 to keep the mentally ill away from the public. Some asylums tried to help the patients. Many did not.

By 1800, England had about 10,000 people who were called "mad". They were put in asylums or "madhouses" where they might be chained to their beds. They were often kept in leg-locks and handcuffs.

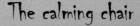

The calming chair

Benjamin Rush was known as the "father of American **psychiatry**". He was one of the first doctors to believe that mental illness is a disease of the mind and nothing to do with **demons**.

Benjamin Rush made a special chair to hold mentally ill patients still.

A drawing showing life in Bedlam Hospital in 1763.

psychiatry   the study and treatment of mental illness
trauma   severe shock and distress

Bedbugs and fleas

Hospital beds were itchy places because fleas and bedbugs lived in the bedding.

Bedbugs are wingless insects that feed on human blood.

Misery

Many new hospitals were built across Europe in the 1600s and 1700s. But it was not easy for them to cope when **plagues** struck.

In 1630 there was a terrible plague in Italy. Over 16,000 people were sent to Milan's 280-bed plague hospital. Sometimes patients had to share a bed with as many as four other people! These beds were usually flea-ridden and filthy. Good levels of **hygiene** were impossible.

Almost 80 per cent of patients died. No one knew at the time that the fleas in the beds bit people and spread the plague.

Bedbugs were common hospital visitors.

Word bank   hygiene   standards of cleanliness

Not enough beds

A great plague hit London in 1665.
Victims had to go to leprosy **asylums**
because the hospitals were full.

Even by 1700, London only had two big
hospitals: St Bartholomew's (opened in
1123) and St Thomas' (opened in 1215).
Two of the city's hospitals are still
named after them today.

In the 1700s, hospitals in Paris, France, were
filthy. Often, more than 800 patients were
packed into one **ward**. The smells were so bad
that staff held sponges dipped in vinegar to
their faces.

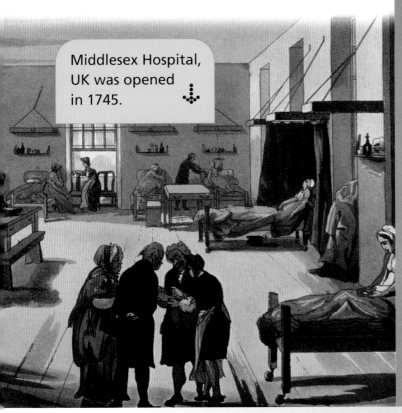

Patients need a
lot of care to stop
their bedsores
becoming infected.

Middlesex Hospital,
UK was opened
in 1745.

Bedsores

Patients left in bed
for a long time can
get bedsores. These
are caused by the
bed and blankets
pressing on the skin.

Seeping bedsores
would have been
yet another misery
for hospital patients
in the 17th century.

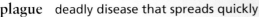

plague   deadly disease that spreads quickly

Dirt

The first hospital in the USA was the Pennsylvania Hospital. Benjamin Franklin and Dr Thomas Bond set it up in 1751 "to care for the sick and **insane** who wander the streets".

The staff kept one noisy patient in the basement. When he escaped and ran up into the attic, no one could get him out. In the end, staff gave him blankets and he stayed there. His nails, hair and dirty beard grew really long. He did not care about the cold or about washing. He never left this small filthy space until he died 7 years later in 1774!

Ward fever

People did not know about **bacteria** 150 years ago. Doctors did not understand how or why wounds poisoned the blood. Doctors and nurses did not wash their hands or their instruments and this led to infection. Ward Fever was a name given to the illness caused by infection.

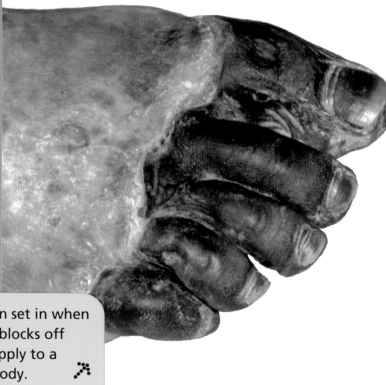

Gangrene can set in when an infection blocks off the blood supply to a part of the body.

22

Word bank **anaesthetic** drugs to make patients sleep or to make treatment less painful

Pain

In the early 1800s some surgeons began to cut open patients. They tried to repair **organs** or remove diseased parts. It was very risky. Chopping off parts of the body would often lead to **gangrene**.

Patients were cut open while they were wide awake. They were strapped down and often given a rag to bite on. If the shock and pain did not kill them, then the bleeding probably did.

It was not until the 1840s that **anaesthetic** was first used. This made operations much safer.

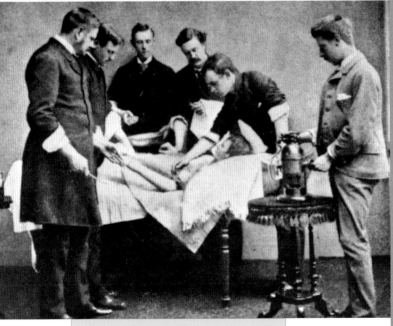

An operation in the late 1800s uses Lister's new antiseptic spray.

Breakthrough

Joseph Lister was a surgeon at a hospital in Glasgow, Scotland. He worried about the number of patients who survived operations but died in the **wards** afterwards. Their wounds turned **septic** and this killed them.

In 1865 Lister found that **antiseptic** bandages helped wounds to heal quickly and safely.

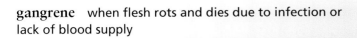

gangrene   when flesh rots and dies due to infection or lack of blood supply

Some hospitals began to set up clinics for **outpatients** to get help. In the mid 19th century many patients used these clinics for advice and quick treatment. Hospitals were no longer just for the seriously ill.

Nurses

Nursing was hard work in the 19th century. Caring for the sick, clearing up mess and washing patients was smelly work. Nurses had to change many stinking bandages.

Yet nurses were not thought to need much special training. In many hospitals, the healthier patients often had to help care for the very ill ones. Nurses earned very little and were treated like servants.

Sisters who ran the **wards** and managed the paperwork had greater respect. Even so, working in a hospital was not often thought to be a good career.

A drawing from 1872 shows an outpatients' clinic.

Word bank

outpatient patient who attends hospital for treatment but does not stay there

Doctors

In the 19th century hospitals became not only places of caring but also of teaching. Student doctors would watch operations. They often had to hold down patients who struggled. But doctors were always men.

The first woman to become a doctor was Elizabeth Blackwell. She had to fight to be allowed to train. At last she **qualified** as a doctor in New York in 1849.

Twenty years later Elizabeth Garrett Anderson worked as the first female doctor in England. In 1872 she opened the New Hospital for Women in London.

Students and nurses discuss a patient at Bellevue Hospital in New York in 1891.

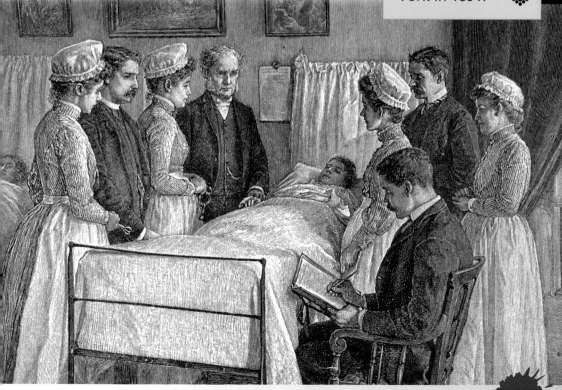

qualified   properly trained, having passed all the tests
sanatorium   place for treatment, rest and recovery

Children's hospitals

Very few hospitals looked after children in the 19th century. A **survey** in 1843 showed there were nearly 2500 patients in London hospitals, but only 26 of these were under the age of 10. At that time, many babies died before they were one year old.

Children growing up in damp **slums** with little food often died from disease. It was not until 1852 that the first hospital for children was opened. It was called The London Hospital for Sick Children.

Then and now

One hundred and fifty years ago, many children died before they reached their teens. Poverty, disease and poor food meant children were often ill.

Today, London's Great Ormond Street Hospital for Children treats 100,000 children every year.

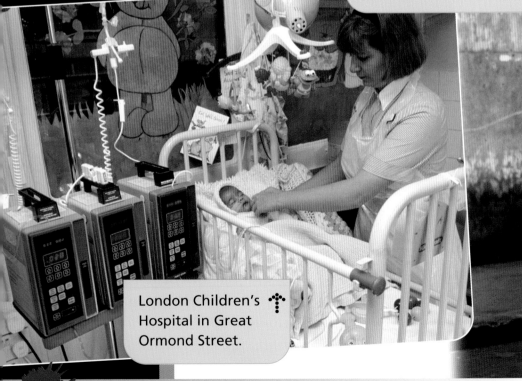

A nurse in 1939 had her own emergency transport!

London Children's Hospital in Great Ormond Street.

Word bank

maternity unit   ward in a hospital where babies are born and looked after

Birth

It is only in the last 50 years that most babies have been born in hospital. Before then they were born at home, with a **midwife** helping at the birth.

During the 1920s, 250,000 American women died giving birth. One reason for this was because midwives were poorly trained.

Today, very few babies and mothers die during childbirth in the USA. This is because of the high standards in modern **maternity units**.

Progress

In 1899, Anna Clise's 5-year-old son died of fever. Anna lived in Seattle, USA where there were no hospitals for ill children.

In 1907, Anna finally persuaded a local hospital to set aside a small **ward** for children. In time this grew to be the Children's Hospital of Seattle.

Fast facts

The first children's hospital to open in the USA was The Children's Hospital of Philadelphia in 1855.

slums   poor, dirty housing in overcrowded parts of a city
survey   detailed study or investigation

In the wars

During the last 150 years more people have been killed and injured in wars than ever before. Hospital staff are often asked to go and work in hospital tents near battlefields.

Crimean War

In 1854, Britain, France and Turkey were at war with Russia. Battles were fought in an area called The Crimea. A newspaper at the time wrote:

> There are not enough surgeons. There are no nurses. There is not even **linen** to make bandages.

A British nurse called Florence Nightingale was determined to go there and help.

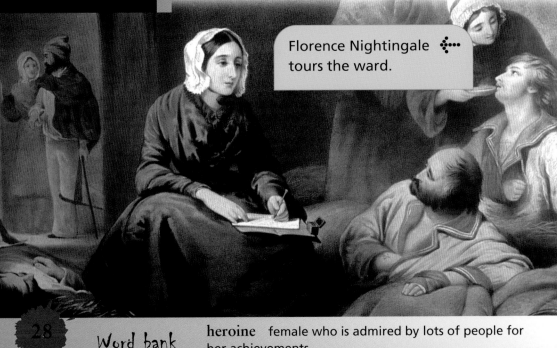

Florence Nightingale tours the ward.

Word bank   **heroine**   female who is admired by lots of people for her achievements

Florence Nightingale

Florence Nightingale went to care for the 2000 sick and wounded soldiers. They were lying in dirty **wards** close to the battlefields. Florence and her team of nurses got to work and cleaned the place up.

Within 6 months the death rate had dropped from about 40 per cent to 2 per cent. When Florence returned home in 1856, she was greeted as a national **heroine**.

Florence Nightingale made women see that nursing was a worthwhile career. In 1860, she started the famous Nightingale Training School for nurses in London.

Mary Seacole

Mary Seacole also went to The Crimean War as a nurse. She was born in Kingston, Jamaica, where she learned how to care for the sick by helping in a nursing home.

On the battlefield the soldiers called her Mother Seacole.

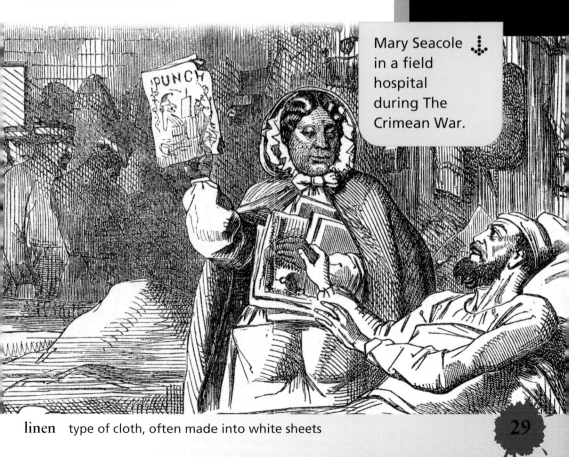

Mary Seacole in a field hospital during The Crimean War.

linen type of cloth, often made into white sheets

American Civil War

In the 1860s, 600,000 men were killed in the American **Civil War**. Up to 75 per cent of them died in field hospitals from wounds or disease. Field hospitals were often just tents in the mud. Doctors could only give basic **first aid** for gunshot wounds.

> **"**At the field hospital, the patients' wounds were dressed, but never with **antiseptic**. Careful hand washing and nail scrubbing was never done before operations or dressing wounds. **"**

Charles Johnson, sent to war on hospital duty aged 18.

Battle wounds

The American Civil War started in 1861. The North and the South could not agree about slaves and how to run the country. Field hospitals were set up in tents close to the battles to deal with all the wounded soldiers.

Long before the American Civil War the only way doctors knew how to treat a bad leg was to cut it off.

Word bank

civil war   when soldiers from the same country fight against each other

A grim business

About 2000 women served as nurses during the American Civil War. They had to clean and bandage bullet wounds that had often become badly infected.

Removing bullets was a messy job. Doctors often caused more infection because they knew nothing about antiseptics.

"When Captain Colby was brought to our hospital he was in a coma from a bullet in his brain. The first thing our surgeon did was to put his finger into the wound, without even washing. Next he used a dirty probe. The patient died a day or two later."

Charles Johnson

Nurse's diary

Many eyes were gazing sadly at us from near the battlefield. I could do nothing for them. As we rode on, the tents of the field hospitals came into view. I gazed in the direction of the battlefield and thought of the nameless dead who were there.

Kate Cumming, a nurse in the American Civil War.

A field hospital in the American Civil War.

---

probe   medical tool inserted into wounds to examine them

In 1863, a Swiss man called Henry Dunant was shocked by the suffering of soldiers in battle. He helped start a medical organization to help in times of war. He changed the Swiss flag with its white cross on a red background, to create The Red Cross.

The Red Cross

In 1863 a group of doctors and nurses met in Switzerland. They wanted to do something to help wounded soldiers across the world.

But they could not risk being shot at while giving medical help on battlefields. They needed a sign to show soldiers who they were. They used the sign of a red cross.

Today the sign of a red cross on a white background means **first aid**, medical help and hospital care.

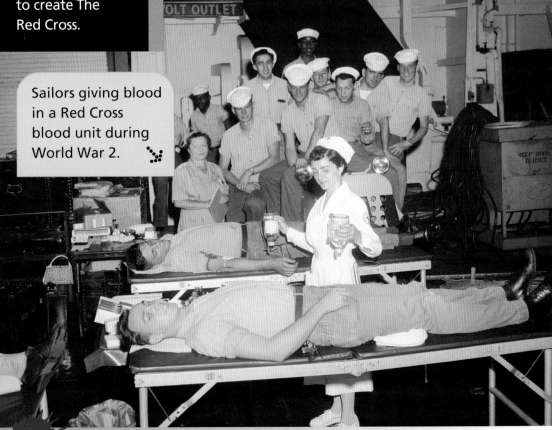

Sailors giving blood in a Red Cross blood unit during World War 2.

American Red Cross

Clara Barton was a teacher from Oxford, Massachusetts, at the start of the American **Civil War**. She went to care for the wounded of both sides.

After the war she went to Europe and learned of the Red Cross organization. She returned to the USA and began the American Red Cross in 1881.

During the Spanish-American War of 1898, Clara Barton helped many women go to battlefields to nurse the wounded. The US Army admitted they would never have coped without the nurses. The Red Cross was here to stay.

Spanish-American War

During the Spanish-American War of 1898, field hospitals in Florida and Cuba were full of disease. The Red Cross sent emergency supplies to help the nurses save lives. It has done this important job ever since, all around the world.

Red Cross nurses did vital work in wartime.

World War 1

No war before World War 1 had killed so many soldiers. From 1914 to 1918, 8 million soldiers died. Many were killed in the muddy **trenches** of the battlefields in France and Belgium. Many more died in the field hospitals.

Doctors had to cut off more wounded and infected limbs in World War 1 than in any war before. **Anaesthetic** and **antiseptics** made treatment far safer than it had been in the American **Civil War**. The Red Cross also provided help.

> **"** Doctors quickly examined the wounded. Bloody dressings and cotton wool lay all over the floor. A large basin was overflowing with bloody water. **"**

Roland Dorgelès, World War 1 soldier.

Canadian soldiers in France, 1916.

A painting from 1918 shows soldiers in a field hospital.

Word bank

trenches   ditches dug by soldiers as shelter from enemy attack

Night and day

Field hospitals were much the same for all the countries involved in the war. There were terrible wounds, cries of pain and too few doctors and nurses. There was mud, **trench fever** and the smell of death. A German soldier in hospital wrote:

An exhausted doctor was dressing wounds. He gave injections and calmly told men what to do. I dragged a dead man's coat on to me and fell asleep. A fever filled my head with strange dreams.

A nurse and doctor attend a patient in Rouen, France in 1914.

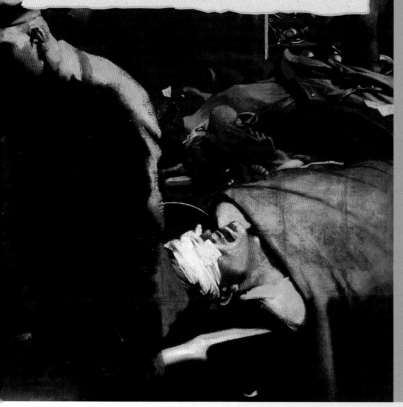

Flu

In 1918 a deadly type of flu began to spread across the world. Of the 1 million US soldiers in Europe, 62,000 died of flu. That was more than the number of US soldiers who died fighting in World War 1.

In the USA the flu killed 675,000 people.

trench fever infectious disease spread in the trenches of World War 1

World War 2

During World War 2, people needed more doctors and nurses than ever before. Aircraft dropped bombs on towns as well as on soldiers. This meant hospitals had to cope with injured **civilians** as well as soldiers.

Field hospitals were set up in tents or any buildings available. In some field hospitals, nurses had to use helmets as washbasins and **bedpans**. Rainwater was collected for washing and drinking. Local herbs were often used to make healing **ointments**.

Medical staff in World War 2 were far better trained and equipped than in World War 1. A wounded soldier's chance of survival was three times higher than in World War 1.

But hospital staff had to deal with terrible burns and **shrapnel** wounds.

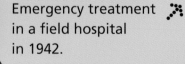

Emergency treatment in a field hospital in 1942.

Word bank

amputation cutting off a part of the body
civilian ordinary member of the public, not a soldier

Disease

Apart from tending to war wounds, field hospitals had to help soldiers with **malaria**. Nurses lined the tents with **mosquito** nets to stop the disease spreading through the hospital. Even so, medical staff also fell ill. One nurse wrote:

> I wish I could forget those endless hours. Hours of giving injections, cutting off clothes and stitching bloody wounds. Hours of **amputations**, settling the patients into their beds, and covering the wounded we could not save. I could not get used to seeing people torn and bleeding like this.

As well as giving medical care, nurses tried hard to cheer up injured patients. An American nurse wrote:

> The words of one badly wounded man were all the thanks we needed. He said, "Are you real? You are wonderful. You are in hell with us."

Posters asked women to join the Red Cross during World War 2.

Join

malaria disease that causes fever and chills, spread by mosquito bites

Wounded troops wait in their bunks on a hospital train during World War 1.

On the move

Mobile hospitals became important in saving lives during war. All major wars have used hospitals that can move from place to place. Soldiers need treatment while they are being moved away from battlefield areas.

As early as 1588, the Spanish **Armada** had hospital ships staffed with 85 doctors. By 1800 the British Navy had 7 hospital ships.

In World War 1, hospital trains or hospital **barges** were used. They were fitted with beds for the wounded as they were moved away from the fighting to proper hospitals.

Wards on wheels

Hospital trains were used during World War 1 to move patients around. They had four or five **ward** carriages and a room for operations. One carriage carried medical supplies, and others carried patients who could sit up. About 400 patients were carried and cared for on each hospital train.

The hospital ship *Argus* in the Gulf War of 1991.

Word bank

armada   large fleet of ships, especially warships
evacuated   removed from a place of danger

State of the art

Today, the US Navy has two huge hospital ships. *Mercy* and *Comfort* were built in the 1980s and were used in the Gulf War of 1991. Each ship holds 1000 beds and has 12 operating rooms. They have the latest medical equipment on board.

The ships have helicopter decks where helicopters land with the wounded. Nine lifts on each ship can each carry six patients on stretchers. Hospital ships have changed a lot since the days of the Spanish Armada!

MASH

During the Vietnam War in the 1960s, the US Army used hospital helicopters. Doctors treated the wounded as they were flown to field hospitals. In this way, 98 per cent of the soldiers who were **evacuated** straight away survived.

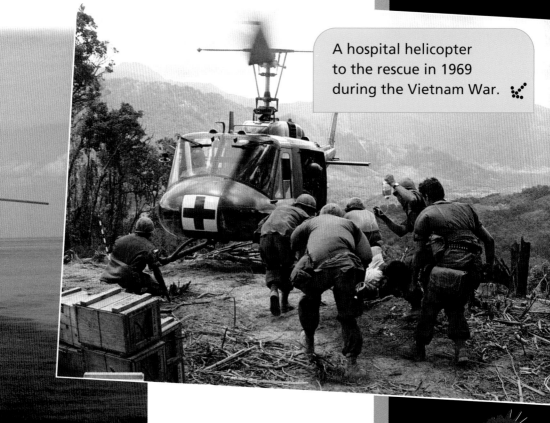

A hospital helicopter to the rescue in 1969 during the Vietnam War.

mobile   can be moved from one place to another

Up to date

Hospitals in the 21st century are nothing like the dreadful hospitals of the past. If you cannot get to a hospital, the hospital can now come to you. Emergency crews today are first-rate medical teams. Their skills and equipment are remarkable.

Australia

Today most of us know where our nearest hospital is. But what if you live a long way from anywhere?

The **outback** of Australia is hundreds of kilometres of desert and bush. People living here used to be in big trouble if they needed medical help. The nearest hospital could be days away.

One of the Australian Flying Doctor aeroplanes.

Word bank

outback   area a long way from any town

Flying doctor

The Australian Flying Doctor Service now brings hospital support to the most **remote** areas. Planes save hundreds of lives each year.

In the 1990s, a family went camping in the outback near Monkey Mia. Their young son, Ryan, seemed unwell. He began to turn blue and was unable to breathe. His parents had to call the Flying Doctor fast.

A pilot landed and quickly flew Ryan to hospital in Perth. He spent five days there being treated. A bad infection had blocked his windpipe. He made a full recovery and is now a healthy teenager.

The African bush

A few hundred small hospitals serve the 20 million people who live in **rural** East Africa. There is only one doctor for every 25,000 people. The East Africa Flying Doctor Service can reach most of these people quickly. It often saves lives.

A flying doctor in Nairobi, Kenya.

remote   far away or distant place, in the middle of nowhere

With all its mountains and rocky coast, New Zealand's air ambulance service is kept busy. In 2001, a special aeroplane was added to the fleet of ambulances. The *Life Flight NZ* can carry two **intensive care** patients at a time.

Air ambulance

Just like the **outback** in Australia or the bush in parts of Africa, most countries have areas far from a hospital. People often need to be rescued from mountains or the sea. This is why helicopters with the latest medical equipment on board are so important today. They carry specially trained flight-nurses to rescue people from places that ambulances cannot reach.

The first helicopter rescue service began in Denver, USA in 1972. By the 1990s, many countries in Europe had their own helicopter ambulances.

The New Zealand *Life Flight* air ambulance.

Word bank   **intensive care**   ward or area where dangerously ill patients are given special care

2003: LIGHTNING STRIKES CLIMBERS IN WYOMING, USA

Lightning killed one climber and threw two others down the Grand Teton peak in Wyoming. They were badly burned and stunned. Night was falling as they hung by ropes from a cliff.

One member of the party used a mobile phone to call for help. An air ambulance rushed to the scene and the climbers had emergency **first aid** treatment during the flight. Then they were taken to the hospital burns unit in Salt Lake City. Fast action saved their lives.

Inside an air ambulance.

HELICOPTER ASSOCIATES

N5779U

A rock climber with a broken foot is rescued by helicopter.

Air hospital

A special hospital plane with full medical equipment and medical staff operates from Beijing airport in China. The hospital plane attempts to deliver the hospital to the roadside.

Emergency

Today, being injured far from a hospital does not mean you cannot be treated.

Eight-year-old Jessie Arbogast was swimming in the sea in Florida in 2001. A large shark bit off his right arm. Jessie's uncle fought the shark until a park ranger shot it.

They pulled Jessie's arm from the shark's throat and packed it in ice. **Paramedics** quickly arrived at the scene and airlifted Jessie to hospital.

It took doctors 11 hours to sew Jessie's arm back on. Today Jessie has some brain damage, but he survived against all odds.

Speed saves lives

Speed is vital when a patient is badly injured. Staff in **A and E** departments or **trauma** centres within hospitals must act quickly.

Paramedics begin life-saving treatment only seconds after arriving at the scene of an accident.

Rescue teams help the injured in Madrid after the terrorist attack on the city in 2004. ···⦂

Word bank

defibrillator   machine that can shock heart muscles into working again after they have stopped

Bomb attack

Sometimes events happen that can put huge pressure on hospitals. In March 2004, **terrorists** blew up trains in Madrid. It was the worst terrorist attack in Spanish history. Nearly 200 people were killed and thousands more injured. Hospitals had to act quickly.

Before long, 1300 emergency workers were helping victims. Over 100 ambulances rushed the wounded to hospitals. Thousands of people hurried to give blood. Hospitals were at breaking point but many lives were saved.

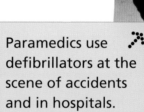

Paramedics use defibrillators at the scene of accidents and in hospitals.

First aid

If the heart stops, the brain does not get enough blood and oxygen. Now, we have a life-saving machine called the **defibrillator**. This can shock the heart back into a regular beat just after it has stopped.

paramedic   emergency worker who gives first aid before and during a journey to hospital

Maggots

Would you believe that maggots are part of 21st-century medicine? They may not be **high-tech,** but they are ideal for treating some injuries.

Maggots eat dead, infected **tissue.** They kill the **bacteria** that stop the healing process and can quickly stop **gangrene** from taking hold. Maggots leave healthy flesh alone so they do your body no harm. Imagine waking up in hospital and seeing maggots wriggling out of your flesh! They might be doing you good, but you would probably be a bit shocked!

Maggots are bred specially for hospital work.

Maggot surprise!

Today, more than 200 hospitals in the USA, UK and Europe use maggots to treat wounds. Bedsores, leg **ulcers** and **surgery** wounds that will not heal by themselves are just right for maggots to work on.

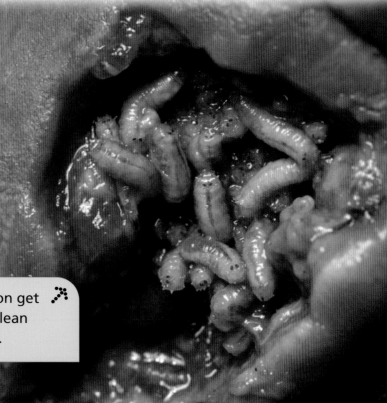

Maggots soon get to work to clean up a wound.

Word bank   **scalp**   skin covering the top of the head, where hair grows

Blood-suckers

For 2500 years, doctors have used blood-sucking leeches. A **leech** can drink blood up to five times its own body weight. It also makes a chemical that stops blood clotting. This can help a patient's blood flow around the body better.

In 1994, a machine ripped off a woman's **scalp**. Doctors at the University of Southern California had to sew it back on. But it swelled with **stagnant** blood. The doctors used leeches to suck out the stagnant blood. This meant that blood could flow back to the patient's scalp and it helped to heal her.

Leeches have been used in hospitals for centuries.

stagnant   still and lifeless
tissue   substance that a living thing is made of

Another world

Once, hospitals could only provide a bed and basic care. Today they have some very advanced equipment. Scanning machines can tell doctors exactly what is going on inside our bodies. Some machines can work our **organs** for us. Heart-and-lung or kidney machines can keep us alive.

Even when patients are dangerously ill, they can be rushed to **intensive care** to be plugged into a life-support machine. This runs their body for them so doctors have a chance to treat the problem.

Computers

Today many hospital doctors carry small portable computers with touch screens. They can connect these to the hospital's main computer system. By tapping on their touch screen, doctors can see a patient's complete medical notes.

Touch-screen computers replace much of a doctors' paperwork.

Word bank

intestine   part of the body that goes from the stomach to the bowel, where food is digested

In the news

Today people travel across the world to go to the best hospitals for treatment. In 2004, a baby from Italy stayed in a Florida hospital for a special operation. It was the first of its kind. Baby Alessia had a serious muscle disease and all her main organs were failing.

Doctors performed a 12-hour operation to give Alessia 8 new organs. She received a new **liver**, stomach, **pancreas**, small **intestine**, large intestine, **spleen** and two kidneys. Alessia would have died without this amazing **surgery**.

Tomorrow's world

It is only a matter of time before all hospitals become completely **digital**. That means no more written medical notes at the end of every bed. Each patient will have a personal bedside computer.

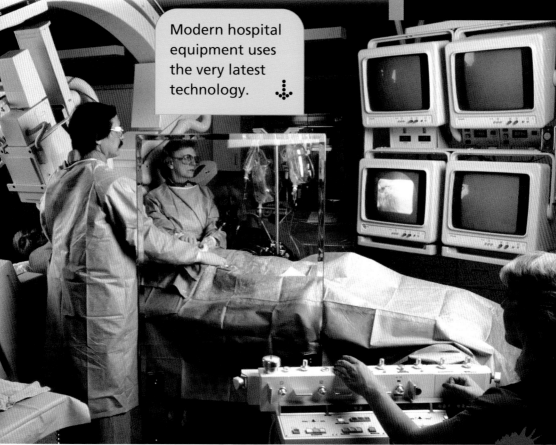

Modern hospital equipment uses the very latest technology.

pancreas   organ near the stomach that controls sugar in the blood
spleen   organ forming part of the immune system

Even though hospitals are full of sick and injured people, they can also be places of laughter. Most doctors, nurses and even patients have funny stories to tell. Some comedy films and TV programmes have been set in hospitals. Can you think why?

Hospital drama

There is something about hospitals that makes us want to see what is going on. Perhaps it is the life and death dramas that happen every day. They certainly make popular TV viewing.

ER has long been America's number one prime time show with a weekly audience of 33 million people. *ER* (Emergency Room) is also shown around the world.

Goran Visnjic (Dr Kovac) and Noah Wyle (Dr Carter) have earned a lot of money acting on *ER*. They have probably earned much more than most real hospital doctors!

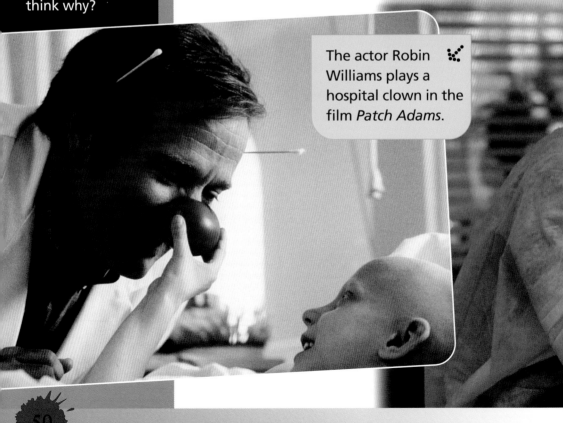

The actor Robin Williams plays a hospital clown in the film *Patch Adams*.

New world

Real life is often more amazing than a TV drama. Imagine waking up in hospital after being asleep for nearly 20 years. You would see quite a few changes.

This really happened to one man. In 2003, Terry Wallis woke from a 19-year **coma**. He was 19 years old when he was in a car crash in Mountain View, Arkansas, USA. He is still learning about the modern world.

Terry's daughter was born just before the crash. She was 19 when her father woke up and spoke to her for the first time.

No real change

Anyone waking up in another 20 years time in a hospital bed is likely to see even more changes. But one thing will remain the same. However much hospitals keep changing, you can bet they will always have plenty of **bedpans**, bandages and blood!

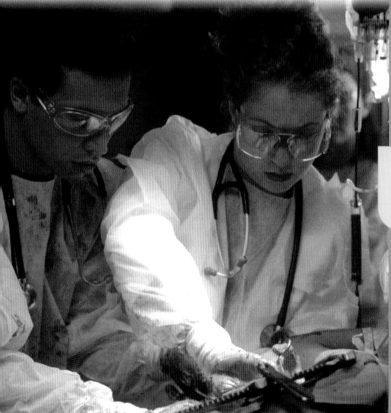

Just another day's work for the stars of *ER*.

Find out more

Did you know?

- The largest blood donation in one day took place in India on 7 December 2003. 15, 423 donors took part, giving the equivalent of 67 bathtubs of blood!

- The longest operation took place in Chicago, USA in 1951. It took surgeons 96 hours to remove a lump from the ovary of Gertrude Levandowski.

Books

Great Inventions: Medicine, Paul Dowswell (Heinemann Library, 2001)

Microlife: Scientists and Discoveries, Robert Sneddon (Heinemann Library, 2000)

The Life and World of: Florence Nightingale, Struan Reid (Heinemann Library, 2003)

Using the Internet

Explore the Internet to find out more about medicine through the ages. You can use a search engine, such as www.yahooligans.com, and type in keywords such as:

- leech
- Florence Nightingale
- gladiators

Search tips

There are billions of pages on the Internet so it can be difficult to find exactly what you are looking for.

These search tips will help you find useful websites more quickly:

- Know exactly what you want to find out about first.
- Use two to six keywords in a search, putting the most important words first.
- Be precise. Only use names of people, places or things.

Glossary

A and E Accident and Emergency

amputation cutting off a part of the body

anaesthetic drugs to make patients sleep or to make treatment less painful

antibiotic substance made from bacteria that kills other harmful bacteria

antiseptic substance that stops harmful bacteria growing and spreading disease

armada large fleet of ships, especially warships

asylum place where people can shelter and be safe

bacteria group of tiny living things; some can cause disease

barge long, flat-bottomed boat, used for transporting goods on rivers and canals

bedpan shallow pan used as a toilet by someone who cannot get out of bed

blood-letting cutting the skin or a vein to let blood flow out

Christian follower of Jesus Christ and the religion based on his teachings

civilian ordinary member of the public, not a soldier

civil war when soldiers from the same country fight against each other

coma like being in a deep sleep, usually caused by injury or disease

defibrillator machine that can shock heart muscles into working again after they have stopped

demon evil spirit or devil

digital storing information in computers

epidemic outbreak of a disease that spreads quickly over a wide area

evacuated removed from a place of danger

first aid help given to a sick or injured person until full medical treatment is available

fort building like a castle, able to withstand enemy attack

gangrene when flesh rots and dies due to infection or lack of blood supply

gladiator Roman trained to fight with weapons

heroine female who is admired by lots of people for her achievements

high-tech using the very latest technology

hostel cheap place for travellers to stay

hygiene standards of cleanliness

infectious spreads easily from one person to another

infirm weak

insane person with mental-health problems

intensive care ward or area where dangerously ill patients are given special care

intestine part of the body that goes from the stomach to the bowel, where food is digested

Islamic relating to Islam, the religion of Muslims

leech blood-sucking flat worm used to bleed patients

leper person suffering from leprosy, a terrible skin disease

linen type of cloth, often made into white sheets

liver organ in the body involved in the digestion process

lunatic name given to a person who was mentally ill

malaria disease that causes fever and chills, spread by mosquito bites

maternity unit ward in a hospital where babies are born and looked after

Middle Ages period of history roughly between AD 500 and AD 1500

midwife nurse who helps women in childbirth

mobile can be moved from one place to another

monastery place where monks live

mosquito tiny fly that sucks blood from animals and people and can spread disease

Muslim follower of the religion of Islam

ointment oily substance rubbed on to skin for medicinal reasons

organ part inside the body that does a particular job

outback area a long way from any town

outpatient patient who attends hospital for treatment but does not stay there

pancreas organ near the stomach that controls sugar in the blood

paramedic emergency worker who gives first aid before and during a journey to hospital

pharmacist someone who prepares and dispenses medical drugs

pilgrim person who goes on a journey to a religious place

plague deadly disease that spreads quickly

probe medical tool inserted into wounds to examine them

prophet religious leader and teacher

psychiatry the study and treatment of mental illness

pus thick yellow or greenish foul-smelling liquid made by infected wounds

qualified properly trained, having passed all the tests

remote far away or distant place, in the middle of nowhere

rural countryside

sanatorium place for treatment, rest and recovery

scalp skin covering the top of the head, where hair grows

septic infected with bacteria

shrapnel fragments of metal thrown out in an explosion

slums poor, dirty housing in overcrowded parts of a city

specialist expert in one particular area

spleen organ forming part of the immune system

stagnant still and lifeless

surgery treating injuries or illness by using cutting and other instruments to operate on the body

survey detailed study or investigation

temple part of the head between the forehead and the ear

terrorist someone who uses acts of violence, such as setting off bombs, to put pressure on a government so that it will do what they want

tissue substance that a living thing is made of

trauma severe shock and distress

trenches ditches dug by soldiers as shelter from enemy attack

trench fever infectious disease spread in the trenches of World War 1

ulcer open sore, often full of pus

ward room in a hospital, normally for a particular type of patient

Index

Titles in the *Painful History of Medicine* series include:

Hardback   1-844-43750-7

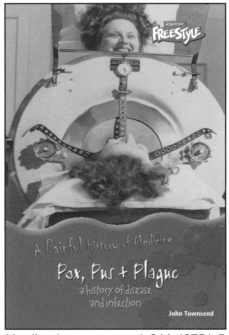

Hardback   1-844-43751-5

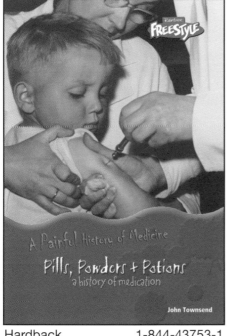

Hardback   1-844-43753-1

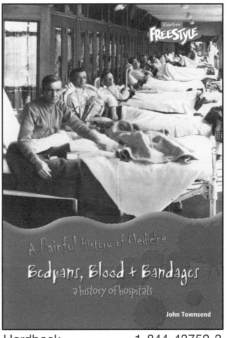

Hardback   1-844-43752-3

Find out about the other titles in this series on our website www.raintreepublishers.co.uk